AF413204

Playing with Pickles

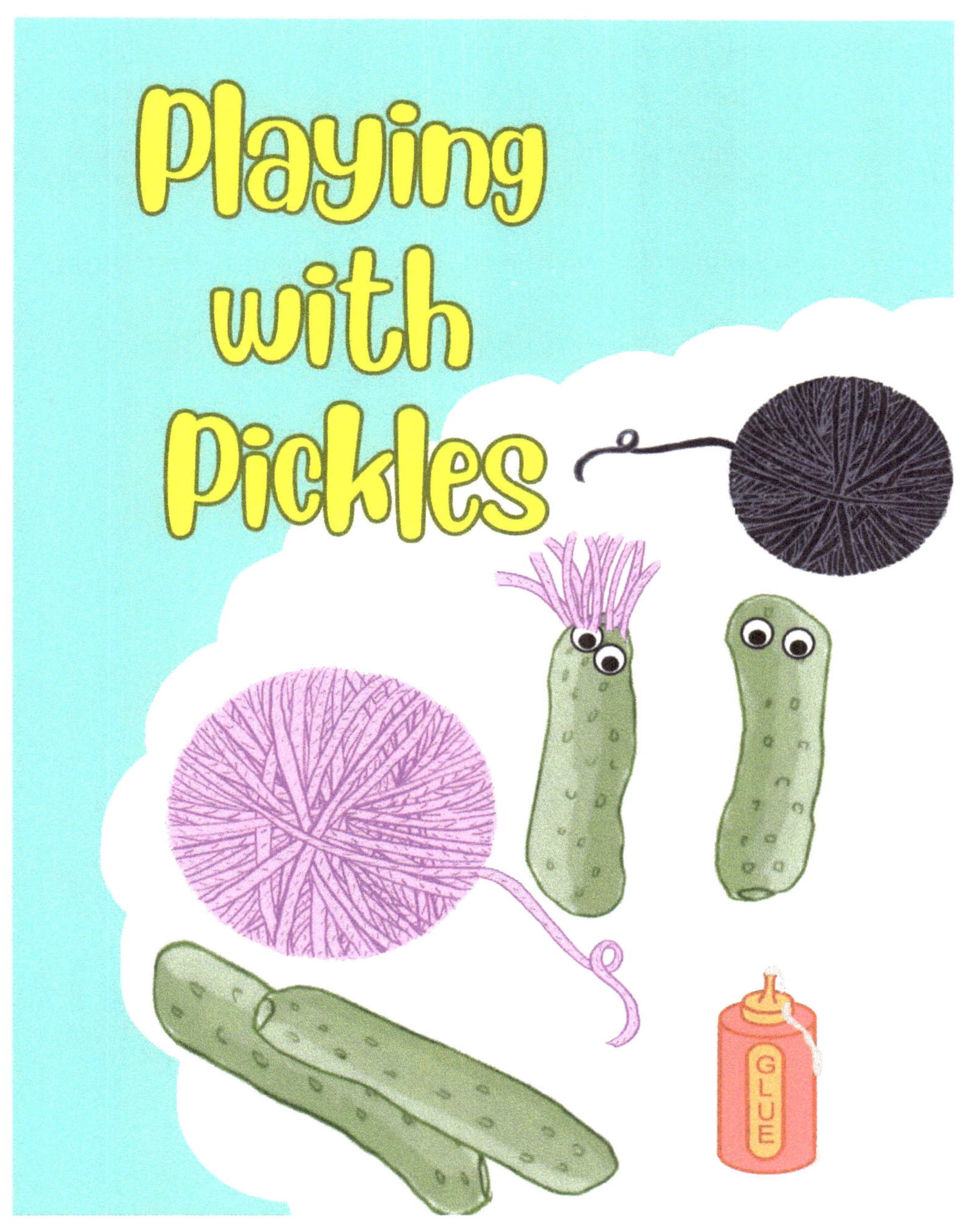

Written and Illustrated
by Gail Jean Murphy

Copyright 2023 by Gail Jean Murphy,

Corel Corporation and its licensors. All rights reserved. No part of this publication may be reproduced, distributed, or tansmitted in any form or by any means, including photocopying, recording, or other electronic or mechanical methods, without the prior written permission of the publisher, except in the case of brief quotations embodied in critical reviews and certain other noncommercial uses permitted by copyright law.

For permission requests, write to the publisher, addressed "Attention: Permissions Coordinator," at info@retrorangerpub.com.

Hidden Hollow Tales, a division of Retro Ranger Publishing Company, Oshkosh, WI.

For Mae & Auz

"Our picnic is nearly ready,"
said Mom.

Chips

"I'll tell the kids it's almost time to go," said Dad.

"Chris! Could you please check on Mae? It's almost time to go!" called Dad.

"I just did! She's upstairs
playing with Pickles,"
said Chris.

"Pickles?!" chuckled Grandma.

"She's really creative,"
answered Grandpa.

"She's practicing her
tally marks," thinks Mom.

"She's practicing her shapes," thinks Dad.

SHAPES

"She's making designs,"
thinks Grandma.

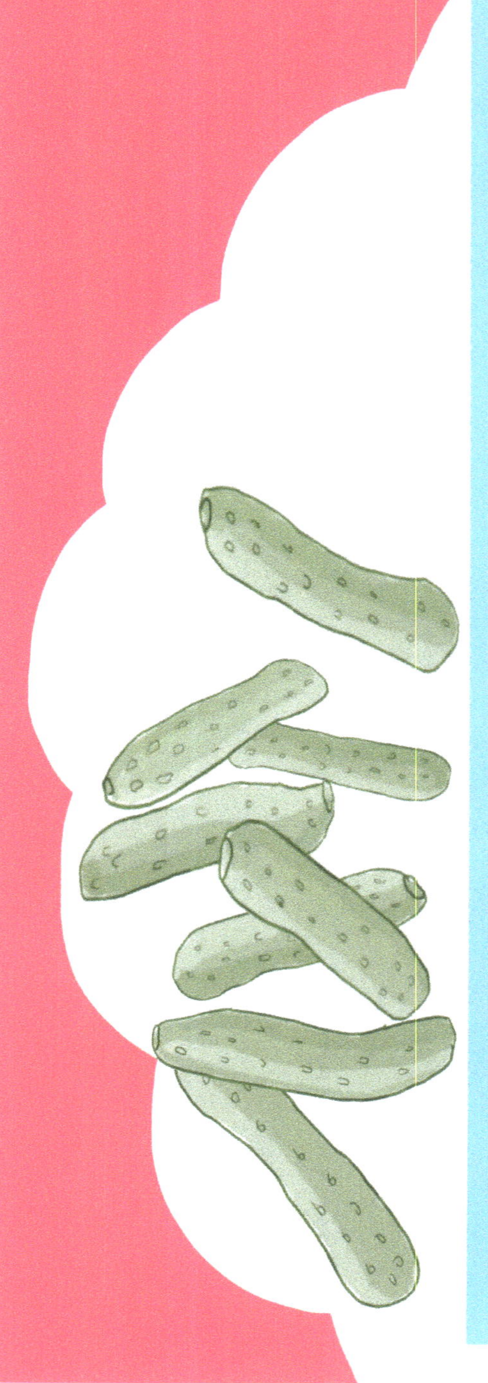

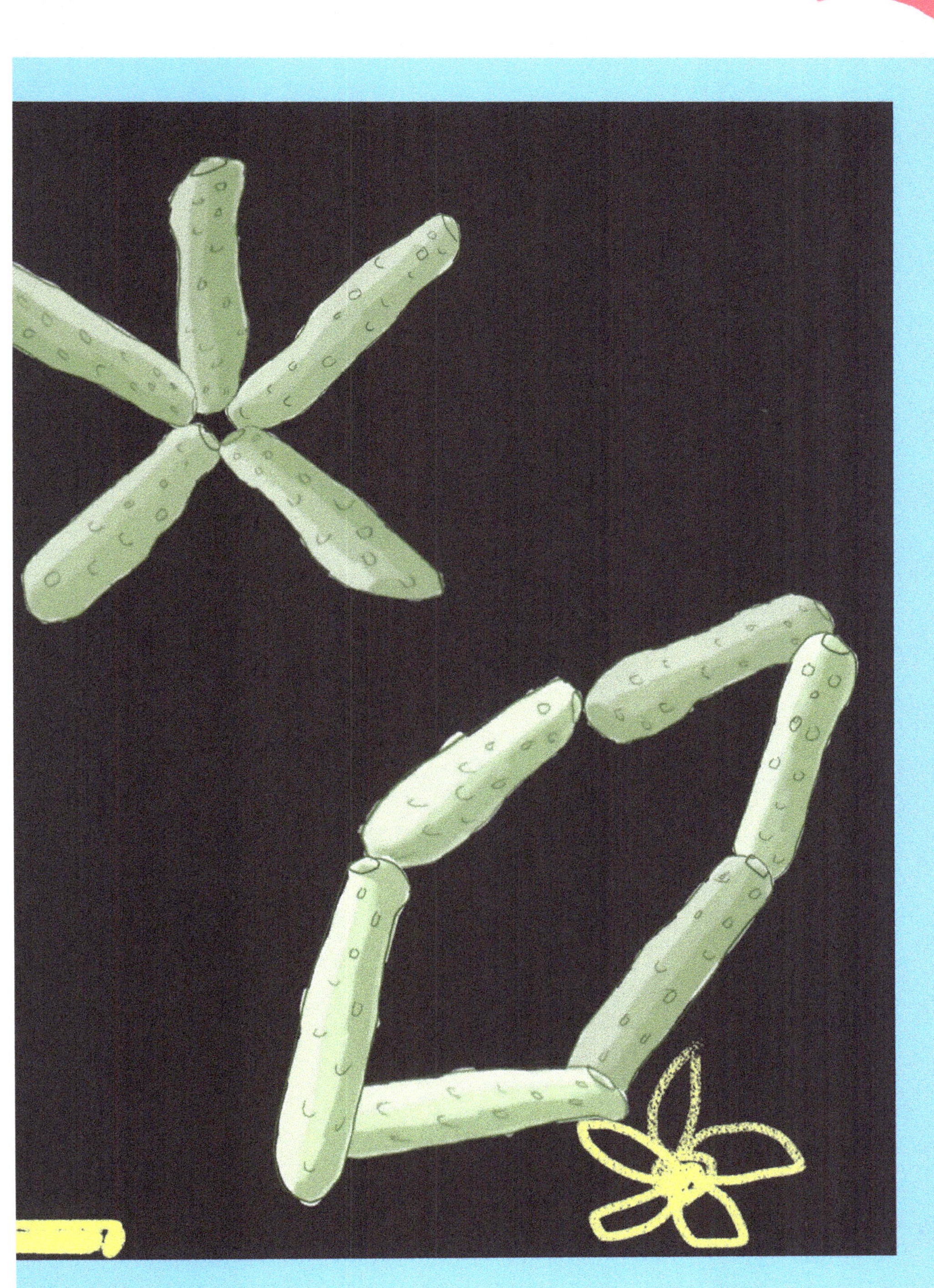

"I bet she's making pickle people,"
laughs Grandpa.

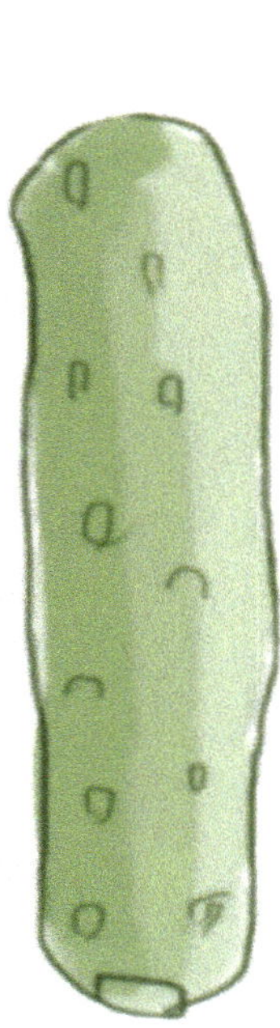

Craft eyes
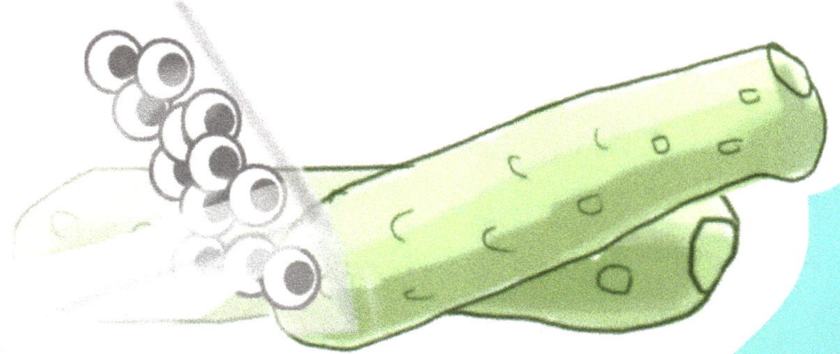

"Or maybe lining them up in rows," thinks Mom.

"She's practicing her letters,"
thinks Dad.

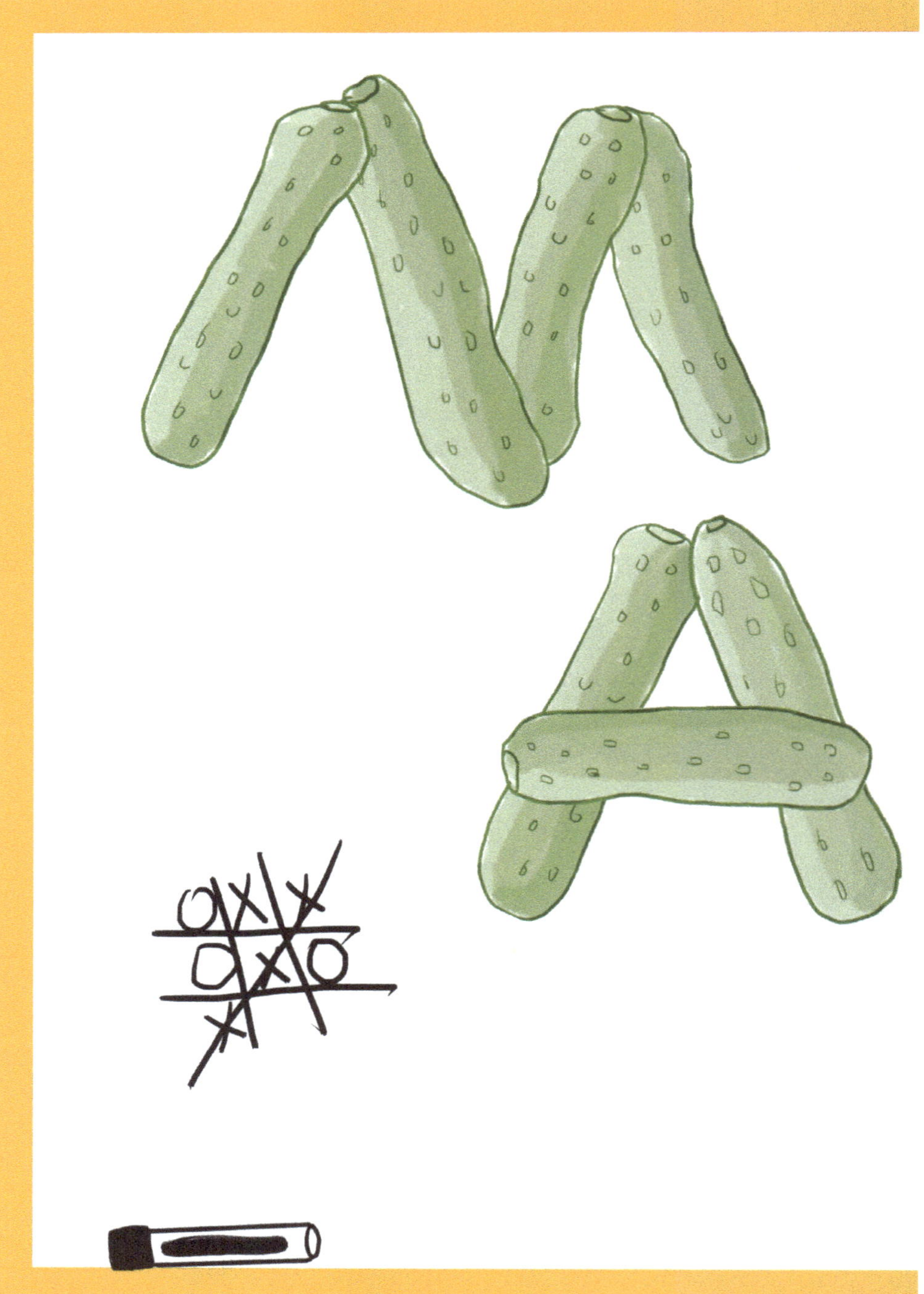

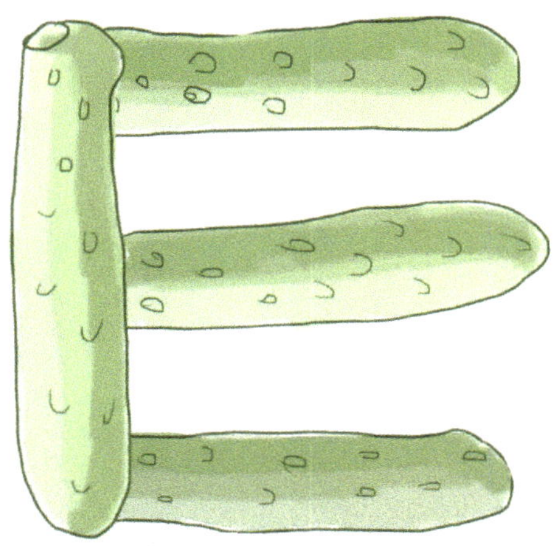

"I bet she's building a castle!"
imagines Grandpa.

"She's building towers,"
thinks Dad.

"Pickle bowling, I suppose," thinks Mom.

BOWLING SCORE

Pickles
Dinosaur Activity Book

Mae

Auz

www.ingramcontent.com/pod-product-compliance
Lightning Source LLC
Chambersburg PA
CBHW040738150726
48196CB00011B/652